NAT TURNER
AND THE
VIRGINIA
SLAVE REVOLT

"I would never be of any service
to anyone as a slave."
∽ Nat Turner ∾
The Confessions of Nat Turner

BY RIVVY NESHAMA

Published by The Child's World®
1980 Lookout Drive, Mankato, MN 56003-1705
800-599-READ • www.childsworld.com

PHOTOS

Cover and page 4: Jacob_09/Shutterstock.com
Interior: Collection of the Smithsonian National Museum of African American History and Culture, Gift from the Liljenquist Family Collection: 10; kdshutterman/Shutterstock.com: 17, 29 (left); Library of Congress, Prints and Photographs Division: 21, 23; Library of Congress, Rare Book and Special Collections Division: 26; Liljenquist Family Collection/Library of Congress, Prints and Photographs Division: 20; Matthew Somerville Morgan/Library of Congress, Prints and Photographs Division: 7, 28 (left); The Miriam and Ira D. Wallach Division of Art, Prints and Photographs: Print Collection, The New York Public Library: 19, 28 (right); North Wind Picture Archives: 8, 9, 13, 14, 24, 31; Schomburg Center for Research in Black Culture, Jean Blackwell Hutson Research and Reference Division, The New York Public Library: 27, 29 (right)

LIBRARY OF CONGRESS CATALOGING-IN-PUBLICATION DATA

ISBN 9781503853720 (Reinforced Library Binding)
ISBN 9781503854048 (Portable Document Format)
ISBN 9781503854161 (Online Multi-user eBook)
LCCN: 2020943352

Printed in the United States of America

Cover and page 4 caption:
A man breaking the chains of enslavement.

CONTENTS

Chapter One

BORN ENSLAVED

This is a story of darkness and light. It tells of a dark, dark time in the history of America. It tells of a time of slavery. It also tells about one man who saw a light in the darkness. What he did helped other people see that light, too. This man's name was Nat Turner. He died for freedom. He was born enslaved.

What does slavery mean? Slavery is when people own other human beings. Slaves are their property, just like a house or horse. Enslavers can make their enslaved workers do whatever they want. And they never have to pay them for their work. Many enslaved people in America lived their whole lives working for their enslavers.

Nat Turner was born on October 2, 1800. He was the "property of Benjamin Turner." Because his mother was enslaved, Nat was, too. Like all enslaved people, he was given the last name of his enslaver. Benjamin Turner was Nat's enslaver.

Nat's mother, Nancy, was born free in Africa. Slave traders stole her from her home when she was just a teenager. They forced her to Southampton, Virginia, and sold her to Benjamin Turner.

Most enslaved people worked on big farms, called plantations, in the South. Plantation owners grew crops of cotton, sugar, and tobacco. Raising these crops took lots of hard work. Many plantation owners didn't have enough money to pay a lot of workers. Others simply wanted to make as much money as they could. To the owners, using enslaved workers seemed like the perfect answer. The workers did all the hard work for no pay at all.

Nat's mother's real name was not Nancy. Nancy was the name given to her by her enslaver. Many enslaved people weren't allowed to use their African names or to speak their African languages. Their enslavers hoped they would forget their homeland and accept their lives as workers. Nancy never forgot Africa or what it was like to be free.

Nancy loved Nat very much. She taught him to love Africa and to be as hungry for freedom as she was. She also taught Nat to hate slavery. That wasn't hard to do. Anyone would hate being enslaved.

The children of enslaved workers like Nat started working when they were only seven years old. They had to rake the yards and work in the kitchen. By the time they were 12, they were working in the fields. They picked crops and took care of the animals all day long.

The children had very little food. They were often hungry. They had hardly any clothes to keep warm. They often had no shoes to wear. At night, they went home to tiny cabins. Many people lived together in these dark, one-room shelters. The cabins had no windows. The floors were made of dirt. The rooms were cold and damp in the winter. Rain leaked through the roofs. Wind blew through cracks in the walls.

Most enslavers lived in big, warm houses. Nat's enslavers, the Turners, were not rich. They often worked with their enslaved workers in the fields. But while Benjamin Turner earned money growing and selling his crops, his workers only got more tired.

The people who were enslaved were told they were inferior—not as good or as smart as the white people who enslaved them. The terrible way they were treated made them feel inferior, too. Enslaved Africans had no **rights** and no power. Their enslavers could control them.

Nat Turner grew up knowing that slavery was wrong, and that enslaved people deserved a better life. Someday, he would lead his fellow slaves in a fight for freedom.

Slavery began thousands of years ago, and it took place in many different countries. Slavery began in North America in the 1600s.

This drawing, called "A Day's Work Ended," shows enslaved workers in a cotton field.

Chapter Two

TO DO GREAT THINGS

When Nat was born, his parents saw that he had certain **birthmarks** on his head and chest. In some parts of Africa, those marks meant that the child was born for a special reason. He was here to help make something great happen. Nat's parents told him this many times as he was growing up.

When Nat was about four years old, something strange happened. He was playing with other children and told them a story. His mother heard him and was very surprised. The story Nat told had happened before he was born! How could he know it? Others were also amazed. They told him that he would grow up to be a **prophet**. They believed he would be a religious leader. They believed that God would speak to him and tell him what to do. Nat never forgot this event and what the people said.

A young enslaved boy sits by the fire in his family's cabin.

Nat and his family likely lived in a cabin much like this one.

There were other things about young Nat that made him seem special. He was one of the smartest children anyone had ever met. Enslavers did not allow their workers to learn to read or write. Still, some people learned to read in secret. Nat was one of them. At that time, even many white people could not read. Nat learned to read when he was very young. Some people say his family taught him, but others say it was the Turners. Benjamin Turner was not as cruel as most enslavers. He always allowed Nat to read. Nat loved to read and find out all he could. He learned from everything and everyone.

Nat's family taught him about the greatness of Africa and the history of his **ancestors**. Nat understood where he came from. He knew he was part of a brave and great people.

Most enslavers did not allow their workers to learn to read because it kept them uninformed. Enslavers believed that educating enslaved people—especially teaching them to read—gave them access to information or ideas that might help them escape.

A poster offering a reward for four fugitive slaves.

Nat worried when his father ran away. He knew that fugitives from slavery were often caught and severely punished. But Nat also understood that freedom was worth fighting for.

Nat was very close to his grandmother, Bridget. She was his father's mother, and she was very religious. Nat and Bridget would read the Bible together, over and over. They read about a time when the Jews were slaves in Egypt. They read that God sent his prophet Moses to lead the Jews to freedom. Nat liked to study religion more than anything else.

When Nat was eight or nine, he learned another important lesson. His father ran away from the plantation. Nat knew that other slaves in the South tried to escape. They tried to get to the states in the North. In the North, many white people believed that slavery was wrong and that it should end. Still, most fugitives from slavery were caught. Then they were punished—or even killed. Nat never knew whether his father found freedom.

As Nat grew older, he learned more and more. While he worked in the fields, he was always thinking or praying. After work, he would read and do experiments. He taught himself to make paper, pottery, gunpowder, and metal.

Other enslaved people began to ask Nat for advice and help. They looked up to him and felt he was different. Nat also felt he was different. So he began to spend a lot of time alone. He would pray for many hours. He would also fast, which meant he ate nothing for a long period of time. Fasting was a way for him to feel closer to God.

One day, when Nat was about 20 years old, he was working in the fields and praying. Suddenly, he heard a voice inside his head. The voice spoke words from the Bible. It said, "Seek ye the kingdom of heaven and all things shall be added unto you." Nat believed he was hearing the voice of the **spirit** that spoke to the prophets in the Bible. He had read many times about the spirit talking to Moses. Now he believed that it was talking to him.

Nat was amazed. For two years, he prayed all the time, even as he worked and rested. Again, he heard the voice and the same words. Nat remembered what he had been told as a child. People had said he was born to do great things. The voice he heard made him believe that this was true. He still did not know just what he was born to do. He would have to wait to find out.

Enslaved workers and their families gathered to play music on banjos and fiddles, and sing songs. The songs told of their sadness and their hopes to be free. Nat heard these "sorrow songs" and sang along.

Chapter Three

THE PREACHER
AND THE PROPHET

When Nat was in his early 20s, many changes came into his life. Benjamin Turner died, which meant that Benjamin's son, Samuel, took control of the plantation and its workers. Times were hard for Virginia farmers. They could not earn much money selling their crops. Some sold their workers to make money. Others hired **overseers** to make the enslaved people work even harder.

Overseers were often cruel men who would beat the workers if they rested at all. Samuel Turner hired an overseer. Right after that, Nat ran away and hid in the woods. No one caught him. Then, after 30 days, he came back on his own.

The other slaves couldn't believe their eyes. Why did Nat come back? Didn't he want to be free? Nat explained to them that he had heard the spirit in the woods. The spirit told him to return.

It reminded him to think of the kingdom of heaven. Some people believe that Nat returned because he was beginning to know what he was there to do. He was not meant to free only himself. He was meant to help free his people.

THE PREACHER AND THE PROPHET

An enslaved man is brutally whipped on a Virginia plantation. The man holding the whip is likely a "driver"— an enslaved man who enforced rules on behalf of the overseer.

Soon after Nat returned, he had a vision. A vision is a dream that people have when they are awake. In Nat's vision, he saw white spirits fighting with black spirits. The sun turned dark, and there was a stream of blood. Nat heard a voice tell him that this was what he would see in his life. It said that no matter how hard this would be, it was up to Nat to live through it.

This woodcut shows the anguish of an enslaved mother as she is taken away from her child.

Some enslavers tried to keep their workers from getting together at religious services. Even so, slaves gathered when they could to listen to a leader speak about God and faith. Listening to preachers tell stories and read the Bible gave them hope.

Nat spent more time alone than ever. He prayed and he fasted. He wanted to make himself ready for whatever he was called to do.

Nat had a wife named Cherry, and they had a son. In 1822, Samuel Turner died. All of his property was sold. A price was put on every piece of furniture, on every farm animal, and on every enslaved person. Nat and his family were sold to different enslavers. Slave families were often separated this way. Nat's wife and son lived on a farm near his. Sometimes Nat could see them.

Nat had more and more visions, which he shared with other enslaved workers. Soon he became a **preacher** to his people. Sometimes he preached at secret meetings in the woods. At other times, he preached at Black churches on different plantations in Southampton. This way, he learned all the secret paths in his neighborhood. He also learned which people he could trust.

People said that Nat was a gentle, quiet man. When he preached, however, he was loud and powerful. He told of the visions he saw and the voice that he heard. He told about the battle between the white and black spirits, and the sun growing dark. He told about **Judgement Day**. The Bible said that on this day, bad people would be punished, and good people would be rewarded. The enslaved workers believed that this meant their enslavers would finally be punished, and the slaves would be free.

Nat's voice rang strong as he told them that Judgement Day was coming! He was preparing his people for something important. He was preparing them to join him once his plans were made.

Many enslaved people saw Nat as their leader. They knew he never drank, smoked, or swore. Some people believed that God spoke to Nat. They called Nat "The Prophet."

There are many verses in the Bible that refer to Judgement Day. Some people of faith take the words very literally. They believe God or Jesus will judge every person who has ever lived. Some think it will last just one day. Others think it will be a period of a thousand years! And some believers think it is just a helpful story or idea, rather than a real day.

In May of 1828, Nat heard another voice. It told him to rise up against his enemies. Nat finally knew what he had been born to do. Like Moses, he would help free his people from slavery. He would lead the terrible battle he had seen in his vision. Nat could think of no way to help his people except through violence. This meant that too many people would be injured or die. In the end, violence would not accomplish Nat's goal. He would not be able to free his people with weapons. Still, he listened to the voice. Nat was patient. He waited.

Three years later, on a sunny day in February 1831, strange things happened in the sky. The sun grew darker and darker, until there was no light left at all. Suddenly, the sky was as dark as night. It was a total **eclipse** of the sun. Some people looked up and thought that the world was ending. Nat looked up and watched the sun darken just as it had in his vision. The sign he had waited for was here! Nat called a meeting with the four men he trusted most: Henry Porter, Hark Travis, Nelson Williams, and Sam Francis.

They made plans for their **revolt**. It would take place on July 4th. On America's holiday of **independence**, its enslaved people would fight for their own independence.

When July 4th came, Nat felt too sick with worry to begin the revolt. He knew that two other big slave rebellions had failed before they even began. Some slave **traitors** had told their enslavers of the plans. The men who planned to lead the revolt were killed by hanging. New laws were passed that made the lives of enslaved people even harder. Nat knew all this. He knew that the revolt could mean death for many people. He also knew that he might die. He was only 30 years old.

A solar eclipse happens when the moon passes directly between the sun and the Earth. The moon blocks the light of the sun from reaching Earth. That's why it looked to Nat as if the sky had grown dark.

On August 13, Nat saw another sign in the heavens. Again, the sky grew dark and the sun turned a strange color. This time, Nat was ready to act. He told his four men to meet him in secret that Sunday, August 21. The man who was called "The Preacher" and "The Prophet" was about to become a **general**.

Chapter Four

GENERAL NAT'S WAR

On August 21, two other people joined Nat and his four men at their meeting in the woods. Their names were Jack Reese and Will Francis. Will had scars all over his body from beatings. Nat asked him why he had come. Will answered, "My life is worth no more than the others, and my **liberty** is dear to me."

This strong wish for freedom was the most powerful weapon these men had. The enslavers had all the money, horses, gunpowder, and guns. Nat's six men had only a hatchet, an ax— and each other. They made plans to start the battle after midnight.

And so the rebellion began. Nat's men moved quietly and secretly in the dark. First they went to the Travis plantation. Nat was enslaved by Joseph Travis at that time. They killed Joseph Travis and his whole family. No one could be left alive to warn the other enslavers.

The seven rebels took four guns and some gunpowder from the Travis house. Then Nat made his men line up and march with their new guns. He made them see that they were soldiers, not criminals. They were fighting in a war against slavery. They were fighting for freedom.

Nat's soldiers moved quickly from plantation to plantation. At each farm, they killed the families that held people in slavery. Then they took all the guns, food, and horses they could find. They also asked all the enslaved workers at each plantation to join them in the fight. Many people were too scared. They knew they could be caught and hanged. Still, Nat's army grew bigger and bigger. They rode from farm to farm throughout the night. They killed more than 55 people.

Nat gathered with his most trusted friends to plan their revolt. On August 22, 1831, they began the rebellion at the Travis Plantation.

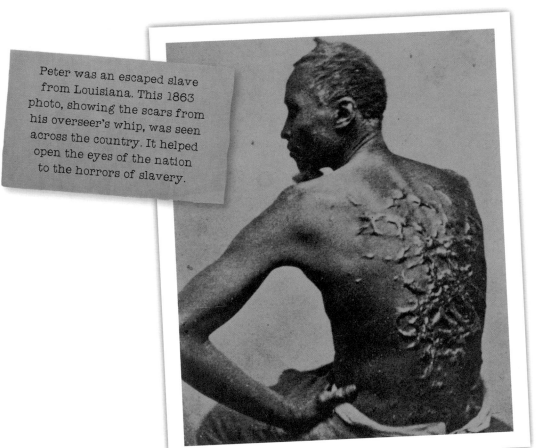

Peter was an escaped slave from Louisiana. This 1863 photo, showing the scars from his overseer's whip, was seen across the country. It helped open the eyes of the nation to the horrors of slavery.

Will Francis had scars all over his body, much like the man in the photo. When Will joined forces with Nat to revolt against the white people who enslaved them, he said he wasn't afraid. Nat asked Will if he thought he would gain his freedom. Will said, "I will, or lose my life."

By Monday morning, Nat's army had more than 60 soldiers. Most had found guns and were riding on horses. They shouted and cheered when Nat rode toward them. He was their general, and they listened to his orders.

Now, Nat ordered his men to ride to Jerusalem. Jerusalem was the main town in Southampton County. Many guns and lots of gunpowder were stored there. Nat also believed that they would find more slaves to join their army in the town. He knew secret paths that led there.

On their way to Jerusalem, Turner's army met a group of 18 white men. They had guns and were on horses. This was the first real battle in Turner's war. It took place at James Parker's farm. General Nat ordered his men to fire and rush forward. They did—and they won.

But there wasn't time to rest. Nat's revolt was no longer a secret. Church bells were ringing in Jerusalem to warn white people to hide and take arms. Many more white men with guns soon attacked Nat's army. Nat saw some of his bravest men get hurt or killed. Some of his men rode away, hoping to escape. Others had been drinking brandy that they had found at the plantations. They were too drunk to fight well.

This collecting card, called "Blow for Blow," shows an enslaved man standing over his white overseer.

Nat could not find enough men to make their way to Jerusalem. So he turned back. He hoped to gather all his men together again later. He was still riding with about 40 of his soldiers. They saw white men with guns wherever they went. They knew that these guns were much more powerful then theirs were. Many of Nat's soldiers were just teenagers, and they had never been taught to fight. There were more shootings, and more of Nat's men ran away. Nat believed that many men had been caught and made to betray him. After two days, Nat returned to the Travis plantation. There, he dug a cave and hid.

By now there were 3,000 white men with guns marching from Virginia and other states to Southampton. Many white people were scared and angry. They wanted **revenge**. The revolt had been more violent than any other uprising before it. Nat wanted enslavers to be scared. He wanted them to be so frightened that they would give up and free their workers. Now, the white army used violence to scare the rebels. They wanted them to be too scared to rebel ever again. So they killed more than 100 enslaved people. They beat and punished many more.

The rebels of Nat's army were caught and put in jail. Many were hanged. But where was General Nat? People all over Virginia were scared that he would fight again. Men with dogs were searching for him. They didn't know he was hiding in a dark hole. At night, Nat would sneak out to find water and food. Then he would hide again.

General Nat had led the biggest slave revolt in U.S. history. He had put together an army of enslaved workers to fight for freedom.

Most enslaved people viewed Nat as a hero. They believed he had the right to rebel. They were proud of his courage. Most enslavers hated and feared Nat. Until they found him, they would be afraid to sleep. While they looked for Nat Turner, they shot more and more enslaved people.

Turner's revolt lasted almost three days. By the time it was over, Turner and his men had killed more than 55 people.

Chapter Five

DARKNESS AND LIGHT

After hiding for six weeks, Nat was caught on October 30 by a man with a shotgun. The man's name was Benjamin Phipps. Nat was taken to a jail in Jerusalem. The judge asked him to admit that what he had done was wrong. Nat said no. He knew that what was really wrong was slavery. He believed that what he did was necessary to make slavery end.

Most of Nat's soldiers were caught right away, but he was able to hide in the woods for six weeks. A reward of $1,100 was offered for his capture. Eventually, a man named Benjamin Phipps caught him.

A white lawyer named Thomas Gray visited Nat in jail. He found Nat to be a man of great intelligence. Nat told him the story of his life and his revolt. Gray later published Nat's story and called it *The Confessions of Nat Turner.*

In his "confessions," Nat said that the reasons for his revolt began with his birth. Although he was born enslaved, he had been born for great things. Nat also told Gray about the voices he heard and the visions he saw. He explained how his revolt was a religious battle. He believed he had done what the spirit wanted him to do.

Nat's beliefs made Gray and some other people call him a religious **fanatic**. They thought he was too religious to see things clearly. They also saw him as a violent man who was full of anger.

Nat's **trial** was held on November 5. He was accused of planning and leading a revolt. Nat had already admitted to all he had done. Still, he said he was not guilty. That's because he did not believe that what he did was wrong. The white judge did not agree. He said that Nat was guilty and would be killed by hanging.

On November 11, 1831, Nat Turner walked to the hanging tree. He looked brave and calm. His faith was as strong as ever. His only words before he died were, "I am ready."

After Nat's death, enslaved workers were treated worse than before. Some were even killed. Most of them were innocent and had nothing to do with the revolt. New laws were passed that made the lives of slaves even harder. They could no longer meet for prayer by themselves. Instead, a white person always had to be with them. The new laws said that no Black person could be a preacher. They said that anyone who taught an enslaved person to read or write would be severely punished.

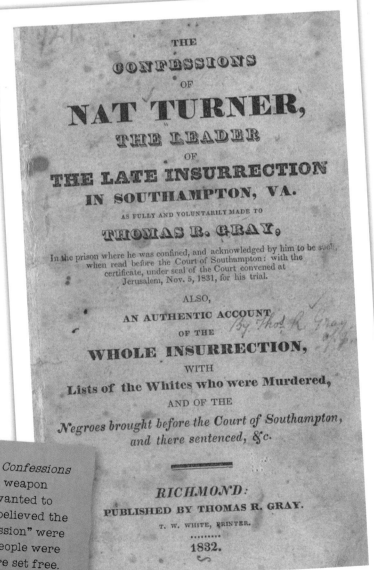

THE CONFESSIONS OF NAT TURNER, THE LEADER OF THE LATE INSURRECTION IN SOUTHAMPTON, VA.

AS FULLY AND VOLUNTARILY MADE TO THOMAS R. GRAY,

In the prison where he was confined, and acknowledged by him to be such, when read before the Court of Southampton: with the certificate, under seal of the Court convened at Jerusalem, Nov. 5, 1831, for his trial.

ALSO,

AN AUTHENTIC ACCOUNT OF THE WHOLE INSURRECTION, WITH Lists of the Whites who were Murdered, AND OF THE Negroes brought before the Court of Southampton, and there sentenced, &c.

RICHMOND:
PUBLISHED BY THOMAS R. GRAY.
T. W. WHITE, PRINTER.
1832.

Some people used *The Confessions of Nat Turner* as a weapon against those who wanted to abolish slavery. They believed the details of Nat's "confession" were proof that enslaved people were dangerous if they were set free.

After Nat Turner's revolt, white people no longer said that people were content to be enslaved. They no longer said that Black slaves would never rebel. They began to see that no one can keep other people enslaved.

Nat **inspired** and led more people—white and Black—to speak out against slavery. Most of these people lived in the North. They were called **abolitionists**. They wanted to abolish, or end, slavery. Nat's actions and bravery also inspired enslaved people to continue the fight for freedom.

An artist drew this sketch of Nat Turner based on people's descriptions of him. Although Nat confessed to all he had done, he still said he wasn't guilty of a crime. He believed the evil of slavery forced him to revolt.

When a person dehumanizes another person, they take away the qualities that make that person human.
How is changing the name of a person dehumanizing?
In what other ways did enslavers dehumanize their workers?

Think about the life and living conditions of an enslaved person.
Why do you think an enslaved person would become
a "traitor" and alert their enslavers to a revolt?

TIME LINE

1600s

Slavery begins in America.

1800

1800
Nat Turner is born in Southampton, Virginia, on October 2. He is enslaved by Benjamin Turner.

1820

1821
Nat hears a spirit telling him what to do and speaking words from the Bible. Nat runs away from the farm of Samuel Turner and then comes back on his own. Nat marries an enslaved woman named Cherry, and Nat has a vision of black and white spirits fighting. In his vision, he also sees the sun turning dark.

1822
Samuel Turner dies. Nat and Cherry are sold to different enslavers.

Nat led an uprising that killed more than 55 white people.
In response, the white people killed more than 100 enslaved people.
What does it say about who has the power when the
"ruling" group uses violence to end an uprising?

Thomas Gray published Nat's story, calling it _The Confessions of Nat Turner_.
Yet this book says that Gray called Nat a "religious fanatic."
As a reader, do think you can trust Gray's book to be accurate and true?

Enslaved people saw Nat as a hero.
Enslavers feared him and thought he should die.
Is either one right? Consider his whole experience
and form your own opinion of who he was.

1860

1825
Nat becomes a preacher.

1828
Nat hears a voice telling him it will soon be time to kill his enemies. The voice says to wait for a sign in the heavens.

1831
A major eclipse of the sun occurs in February. On August 13, Nat sees another sign in the heavens. On August 22, Nat and his men begin the slave revolt. It lasts for a few days before state and federal troops stop it. Nat hides for nearly six weeks before being captured on October 30 and taken to jail. Nat tells his "confessions" to lawyer Thomas R. Gray on November 1. Four days later, Nat goes to trial and is found guilty of planning and leading a slave revolt. Nat is hanged in Jerusalem, Virginia, at the age of 31.

1865
The American Civil War ends in April. Slavery is officially ended by the 13th Amendment to the Constitution at the end of the year.

GLOSSARY

abolitionists (ab-uh-LISH-uh-nists)
Abolitionists were people who worked to end (abolish) slavery. Nat Turner inspired many abolitionists.

ancestors (AN-ses-terz)
Ancestors are someone's family members who were born long before, such as grandparents or great grandparents. Nat Turner's ancestors were from Africa.

birthmarks (BERTH-marks)
Birthmarks are marks on the skin that people have when they are born. People told Nat Turner that his birthmarks meant he was going to do something important in his life.

eclipse (ee-KLIPS)
During an eclipse of the sun, the moon comes between the sun and the Earth. When this happens, the moon blocks part or all of the sun's light, so the Earth's sky grows dark.

fanatic (fuh-NAT-ik)
A fanatic is someone who always talks or thinks about something they like or believe. Some people called Nat Turner a fanatic because of his strong religious beliefs.

general (JEN-er-el)
A general is an important army officer who tells soldiers what to do. People called Nat Turner "General Nat."

independence (in-dee-PEN-dentz)
Independence is freedom. July 4th, known as Independence Day, is the U.S. holiday that celebrates the nation's independence.

inspired (in-SPIYRD)
An inspiration is someone or something that encourages a person to do good things. Nat Turner inspired generations of African Americans.

Judgment Day (JUDJ-ment DAY)
Some people believe that Judgment Day is a day when all bad people will be punished by God and all good people will be rewarded. Nat Turner told other enslaved workers that Judgment Day was coming, and that enslavers would be punished.

liberty (LIB-er-tee)
Liberty means freedom. General Nat and his soldiers wanted liberty.

overseers (oh-vur-SEE-urz)
In the time of slavery, an overseer was someone whose job was to make the enslaved people work very hard, often by being cruel. Nat Turner's enslaver hired an overseer.

preacher (PREE-chur)
A preacher is someone who gives a religious talk to people. Preachers often give talks at church services.

prophet (PRAH-fit)
A prophet is a person who is believed to speak for God. A prophet can also be someone who tells the future or is a religious leader.

revenge (ree-VENJ)
Revenge is doing harm to someone who has harmed you. White people wanted revenge after Nat and his soldiers rebelled.

revolt (ree-VOLT)
A revolt is a fight against people in power. Enslavers worried that the people they enslasved would start a revolt if they had weapons.

rights (RYTZ)
Rights are the things that the law says people can have or do, such as the right to vote or to practice religion. Enslaved Africans had few rights.

spirit (SPEER-it)
A spirit is something or someone that cannot be seen, but is heard or felt. Nat believed that a spirit talked to him.

traitors (TRAY-turz)
Traitors are those who help the enemy of their own people. Enslaved workers who warned the enslavers about rebellions were viewed by the rebels as traitors

trial (TRY-ul)
A trial is a process used to decide whether a person is guilty or innocent of commiting a crime. Trials take place in a court of law.

BOOKS

Alexander, Richard. *The Transatlantic Slave Trade: The Forced Migration of Africans to America*. New York, NY: PowerKids Press, 2016.

Grady, Cynthia. *Like a Bird: The Art of the American Slave Song*. Minneapolis, MN: Carolrhoda Books, 2016.

Meadows, James. *Slavery*. Mankato, MN: The Child's World, 2021.

Nelson, Kadir. *Heart and Soul: The Story of America and African Americans*. Solon, OH: Findaway World, 2019.

Roxburgh, Ellis. *Nat Turner's Slave Rebellion*. New York, NY: Gareth Stevens Publishing, 2018.

Schmid, Katie Kelley. *Nat Turner and Slave Life on a Southern Plantation*. New York, NY: PowerKids Press, 2014.

WEB SITES

Visit our website for links about Nat Turner and the Virginia Slave Revolt:

childsworld.com/links

Note to Parents, Teachers, and Librarians: We routinely verify our Web links to make sure they are safe, active sites—so encourage your readers to check them out!

INDEX